Also by **KEVIN POWELL**

D0167117

In The Tradition: An Anthology of Young Black Writers
(1993; edited with Ras Baraka)

recognize
(1995; poetry by Kevin Powell)

Keepin' It Real: Post-MTV Reflections On Race, Sex, and Politics
(1997; essays by Kevin Powell)

Step Into A World: A Global Anthology of The New Black Literature
(2000; edited by Kevin Powell)

Who Shot Ya? Three Decades of Hiphop Photography
(2002; Photographs by Ernie Paniccioli/Edited by Kevin Powell)

Who's Gonna Take The Weight? Manhood, Race, and Power in America
(2003; essays by Kevin Powell)

Someday We'll All Be Free
(2006; essays by Kevin Powell)

KEVIN POWELL

NO SLEEP TILL BROOKLYN

New and Selected Poems

Soft Skull Press
Brooklyn

Copyright © 2008 by Kevin Powell.
All rights reserved under International and Pan-American Copyright
Conventions.

Library of Congress Cataloging-in-Publication Data

Powell, Kevin
  No sleep till Brooklyn : new and selected poems / Kevin Powell.
     p. cm.
  ISBN-13: 978-0-9796636-9-7
  ISBN-10: 0-9796636-9-5
  I. Title.

PS3566.083253N6 2008
811'.54—dc22

                                    2007046765

Book design by Kerry DeBruce
Cover photo by Renaldo
Printed in the United States of America

Soft Skull Press
An Imprint of Counterpoint LLC
2117 Fourth Street
Suite D
Berkeley, CA 94710

www.softskull.com
www.counterpointpress.com

Distributed by Publishers Group West

10 9 8 7 6 5 4 3 2 1

R0431091591

For Tracy Alexander and April Silver, two true friends for life, and two of Brooklyn's finest....

So that you will hear me
my words
sometimes grow thin
as the tracks of the gulls on the beaches.

—Pablo Neruda

CONTENTS

KEVIN POWELL

Poet's Note

The following poems were written between 1988 and 2008, from my early days as a poet, to the present. During that span I have gone from a versifier who regularly participated in slams, open mics, and featured readings, to someone who has opted to write poems privately, away from what is commonly called "the scene." Perhaps that is why this, my second poetry collection, took so long to appear (my first was published in 1995). I needed the time, the space, to relearn why I love poetry so much, why I write, why I breathe. So here are 51 poems—42 new pieces, 9 pieces from my previous collection, *recognize*—all equally important to me. The title, *No Sleep Till Brooklyn*, is borrowed from the Beastie Boys' song from their 1986 debut album, *Licensed to Ill*. I humbly thank you for taking the time to read this volume.

Part I. struggle

struggle

Nobody said
this life would
be easy—that it
would take
shooting hot hate
into our blue veins
to smother the
archaic wails
of people
sprinting from
steel gangplanks
to iron waters
to cotton trees

Nobody said
that those cotton trees
would hang us
by our eyeballs,
demanding us to look
at the soul sores
pockmarking
our red, restless rivers

Nobody said
this life would
flow like a red, restless
river, or that that red river
would be an unhurried suicide:
as unhurried as molded syrup
crawling, like a cockroach,
down the face of a
nameless
junkie who gums death
because life has blown
his teeth away

Nobody said
we couldn't smile
anymore; or that
a smile, now, had
to be a wooden mask
forged with the blood
of a face we cracked open,
like a watermelon,
this morning in the mirror

Nobody said a face
like yours is but
a face like mine:
a wrinkled roadmap
slouching toward
a mother, a father,
who have never
hung themselves
with love, who
never pulled their
parents from that
spiritual wreckage
called history, who
never asked the
dead for relief,
and who never, never
pondered why ghosts
who don't smile
wage their civil wars
between our bone
and our flesh

Friday, September 18, 1998
6:06PM

Might it be, as my mother said to me on this ugly, sinful day,
That the world is on its last go-round?
Hijacked wild birds strip the sky of its innocent morning breath
Steel towers crumple like playing cards on an uneven metal table
Unrehearsed screams we dare not hear leap from windows
Into the open, bottomless palms of God
I cannot stand to watch life reduce
Itself to powdery dust and soot lathering the devil's inflamed mouth
But I am fixated on the television anyhow:
Is this what slavery was like?
Is this what the holocaust was like?
Is this what famine is like?
Is this what war is like?
Is this how you felt, dear mother, when King and the two Kennedys were killed?
I want to stitch up the sky, deny humans the right to fly
Cry until my tears have washed hatred
From the mildewed underarms of history
And I want to say to the firemen
Ah, yes, the firemen:
Your husband, your father, your brother, your uncle, your friend
Thank you for speeding to the end of
Your time and thank you for showing us that
Courage is a soul so unselfish it would
Scale a collapsing building to liberate a stranger
Even as your blood relatives wonder if you are alive—
From the remains of this madness
I detect a heartbeat called life
From the remains of this madness
I smell an aroma called love
From the remains of this madness
I embrace a body called humanity
From the remains of this madness
I construct a dream called hope
From the remains of this madness
I will ride the wings of the deceased
Into the clouds, scribble their names on the sun,
Erect a memorial to the moon, chant the blues
For New York City, then resurrect a world
Where a new-born rose will jut through the broken concrete.

November 2001

Rican & Soul

for Tony Medina

It is the twenty-first century and you are now born
    a sensitive Puerto Rican boy from the Bronx
    where boricuas and morenos
    crazy glue their cardboard realities on walls and borough-plated horses,
    use fire hydrants as air conditioners, play cee-lo like it is the opening bell
    at the stock exchange, and
    dodge the police the way cucarachas dodged
    our grandmothers' two-dollar plastic slippers
This is suppose to be a poem about your deceased father
    but it is really about you, amigo
    for you are like macaroni and cheese y arroz con pollo
    mashed at the bottom of a corroded aluminum pot
    the way we were spread like crushed flesh
    in the hulls of slave ships
    the way we salsa with bombs and cancer in vieques today
This just means you got soul
    the way Tito Puente got soul
    the way James Brown got soul
    the way every afro-familia in new york city
    with a relative named Malik Rodriguez or Maria Jackson
    got a little rican and a little soul, nahmean?
But what is behind that soul?
    what must it be like to know that wiseguys
    with names like Columbus and Cortes ordered the massacre
    of natives took the minerals mixed and matched the oppressed
    call you spic call me nigga call us other
    and raped our mothers in their foreheads with heroin needles?
Do you recall your public confession about being
    left in that hospital upon birth?—your oral history of fathers and mothers
    who are black brown tan red yellow
    with the anxieties that their children's lives
    will be them jumping over tombstones
    into the jaws of a waiting inferno? was your
    father one of those children? was his stroke pre-ordained
    the way it seems our lives are pre-packaged to be
    one long clash with the devil?
And if there is truly a god why does the devil always win, hombre?
    why do grandmothers
    who loved us have to die before we are able to punch holes in the

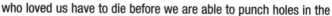

sugar hills like Toussaint, like Che, like Miky Piñero? why did our abuelas
die before they could taste and season the gold dust
flaming the rice and beans in their linoleum kitchens?
Why do our candles puke asbestos fumes, why do our crosses exist inside the
off-white lint lassoing the televised
reruns of our childhood? is it possible that we are
all born with asthmatic hearts and that we spend our entire
lives trying to sanitize the throbs flushing our minds?
Is that what this is all about? tu sabe? what, yo, was your
father trying to tell you at the end, of life, of death,
of mechanical police officers who run over Latino
families in Brooklyn, who offhandedly chuck 41 darts
at an escaped African in the Bronx?
Are we not all escaped Africans? is freedom, then, that mountain Jennifer Lopez
shakes like a sacred bell? or is freedom the machete Willie Perdomo uses
to hack his own lips so that he can speak with the dead on 125th Street?
is freedom Lee Quiñones beating down goliath with aerosol clouds
and throw-ups emanating from the mouths of manifest destiny?
or is freedom Rosie Perez starring as the butter-pecan queen of the jungle
while Hollywood locks the American she in the music
videos of Jay-Z and Fat Joe?
All of this is about fire escapes and fast exits from deathrow, todo dia....
so maybe your father, the old trickster he was, too was escaping—
so maybe your father knew that santeria means
"Mira, chico, you gots to put it on them before they put it on you"
Entonces, your father is not dead, Tony
I swear I just saw him at the bodega copping some Trident gum and
loosies/I swear I just saw him in you, the man inside the boy inside the
man racing against himself, a uniball and notepad in one hand
a gust of wind in the other as the wild strands of his wild existence
draw sand in the line of time
A Puerto Rican man with no country in a country that
says "Rican or soul, it don't matter
because we will never acknowledge how it feels
to be shipwrecked, upon birth, in this cemetery
we named the ghetto"

Friday, August 17, 2001

1:31AM

HairStories

I remember when ma use to take me to the
barbershop when I was little
we ain't had no money so we only
went but once a month
ma would tell the barber to cut it
real close 'cuz this haircut need to
last awhile   seem like every other
boy in the neighborhood had a
mess of hair up on his head
but ma had me damn-near bald
with a razor-thin part on the side
and talcum powder pasted to the back of my neck
one thing I noticed about those
haircuts was how the barber
an old leather-brown black
man with slicked back wavy hair
like an Indian or an Italian would shoo my ma away
when she tried to pay him   he
never said nothing but he must've
known my ma and me was real poor
even though my ma knew what was
going to happen each trip to the shop she dutifully pulled the
time-worn bills from her plastic purse anyway
don't know if anyone else in the barbershop ever saw
that but I sure as heck saw it   that barber kicked the bucket
when I got to be a teenager but I certainly
remember him, and his wavy hair   I wanted
wavy hair just like that   use to think ain't nothin'
in the world like good wavy hair   did not
want my hair 'cuz it was nappy   not real nappy
like some of the other black folks I know
but nappy enough that I was not feeling too good
about my round dome   when I got to be
about 13 ma let me choose my own barber and
do my own thing to my hair   I was working
now and had some change in my pockets
and felt like a big man
heck, I wanted to be a big man
I wanted to be a star—

and I loved the way them stars' hair
looked in them magazines and in them movies
and what not   why I thought the way to let folks
know you is a star is by straightening your hair,
or making it curly, or something that made it good
hair   lawd knows I wanted good hair real bad, yessuh
would stand in the mirror for an hour at a time solemnly
scooping chunky globs of that magic waving cream
into the palms of my hand and rubbed it into my head,
all over, real firm, 'til my fingers nearly stuck together
and damn-near stuck to my head then I would
take that brush, the kind ya use to shine shoes with,
and brush my hair forward, then backward, then
forward again, then backward   I would brush
so hard my scalp would pulsate with pain
pain like ya feel when someone is beating ya
with a tree branch or a mulewhip and then I would tie
that stocking cap around
my head real tight, so tight I would wake up with
a headache and a crease pierced into my forehead
that crease was like a religious marking on
my forehead meant ya was willin' to sacrifice
sleep and comfort to achieve ya objective, ya know?
I did not mind the loss of sleep and the lack of comfort
because I was determined to have good hair   don't remember
much about them years except those headaches
and them creases on my forehead and the fact
that my hair never quite looked like them stars'
hair in them magazines and them movies   when I became
a man for real is when I first began to realize I did not
like my natural hair much at all   felt, all them years,
that my natural hair was ugly,
dirty, a waste of good head space   don't know what
began to change me exactly but maybe it was them
books I began to read, about me and my history,
and I began to see things differently now   I started
loving my natural hair and wearing it in all kinds of
shapes and sizes, picking it up and out the way an
ancient farmer with semi-broken, arthritic fingers

would pick a watermelon or sweet potato
up and out of the earth   yessuh, I suddenly saw my hair
as one with the earth, that it was extraordinary like the earth,
like the sun, and that is why my hair, our hair, in its
natural state, shot straight up to the sky, to the sun
it took a spell for me to love my hair, our hair, completely
can't make a people hate themselves and they hair
and expect that to change overnight   my ma say to me
repeatedly ya use to look decent and now ya look like
trash wearing ya hair like that   ma look at my friends
wearing their hair natural and smirk   she say them
fools think they in Africa or somethin' they need to
look neater and cleaner they need to get them kinks out
they hair   tell ma ain't nothin' neater
and cleaner than to go to a barbershop and ya barber
be like a sculptor molding your head into a royal
crown as you direct him with your ancestor's scissors—
ma look at me and smirk again, talking about ya need
to go ahead with all that fool talk—   ma like the way
I wear my hair now, as a fully grown man   say it
remind her the way she used to have it cut when
I was a little boy   yes, lawd, I done migrated along them railroad tracks to the
tempos of florida water and gideon's trumpet
and I am back to what
we call the low-boy style: the barber digs into my head
like he performing surgery, or a Yoruba ritual—
got his mojo in them spraycans, got his cigar and his drum smacks wrapped in
that foil, got his spirits in his hip pocket, got his clippers buzzing with the bass
player, got his chewing gum hopping between keyboard chomps, got his short
broomstick and the cardboard dustpan, got his chants and moans as he brushes
and combs, and he spins me around in that chair so that the mirror can bless my
head from every dimension   he clamps my head with his left hand, then his
right he talks about the events of the day
offers his unproven analysis, gives me advice on my up
and down love life, and relieves me of my blues
as he cracks jokes, takes one too many bathroom
breaks, and tells that same customer who is always
after me every saturday that he should go find another
barber if he ain't got the patience to wait

ma don't know that the barbershop got a hidden
meaning for us black men, that it is like a secret society
with a coded language—the wink, the head nod, the
tap on the shoulder, the jive talking in tongues—ma don't know she started
something when she brought me here as a boy   that I need this space
and this place like I need the holes in my nose   that
if I did not have this weekly trip to the barbershop
I might not have anywhere else, in this universe,
to be a souped-up, freedom-loving butterfly with nappy locks—

Friday, August 1, 2003
7:21PM

K E V I N   P O W E L L

HairStories

9

Haiku 4 Badu

like billie you are
a field hand picking strange fruits
from those dead tree limbs

Saturday, March 7, 1998
2:05PM

Soul Interlude

I.
i could have been billie holiday
dissecting that microphone
with a glass of cheap gin;
the blues come so easy
when the sky is embittered
from graffiti marks.
someone has etched the warning of george orwell:
remember the numbers, they must be
reversed
else time will have to teach itself to move

II.
a mouth is propelled by a language
i do not understand
the tongue
reddish-purple, bent at the gut
wags like a flag
saluting its neighbor

III.
it is a surrealistic longing:
to sleep inside the drunken head
of edgar allan poe
the tell-tale heart
ah yes,
it punches the floor
it bleeds irony
it sulks at my disobedience
it moons the sun

IV.
a spirit comes over me
s/he covers my dream
with an antiquated cobweb
i cannot move
but words fill the bowl of my throat
i want maternal protection
alas, my mother, she is gone—
the creases in her sheets
have finally captured her

Pre-Millennium Tension

the Toshiba has a black line going across the middle
and the satellite channels are off because I cannot afford
to pay the bill. no matter, I did not really want to watch
Dick Clark tonight, anyhow. but it would have been nice
to peep one pigskin war in the trenches of my living room.
me and buccaneers and eagles and broncos and poe's ravens
co-counseling each other, that body blow—in the back snagged like
a comma,—
as incidental as the warm mucus smoothing my manhood into place.
these days the computer hard drive is full so I must save everything, including
this poem, onto a disk. the desk clock's battery has died. when the
new year erupts my clock will say it is still 1:27A.M. on
whatever day it stopped. my bedroom telephone is deceased,
too, the message alert blinking, for the past eight months, like
a searchlight in the Pacific. does my grandmother's photo, there
on the makeshift altar, wonder how long I have been stranded
in this bedroom—me and the sports section of the *New York Times*?
the biggest snowstorm in the past five years has covered New York City like a
vengeful white ghost. oh, the ghost's kenneth coles are polished with poverty:
mine. for I have but twenty dollars and many many coins
with which to bring in the millennium. ten years in New York
City and I have come full circle back to the b-boy who fled
New Jersey for a better life. at least I have slowed
the pulse of my ambitions and am now content to
live, as Connery does in that movie, somewhere
between infamy and the two fingers snowboarding down my throat.
my apartment, like Connery's, a hole for a bicycling bear with no love to speak
of. my apartment...yes my dear sanctuary...it is
cluttered: half-written poems here; old magazines
there; garbage bags, like lifeless, airless balloons, everywhere;
unpaid and unopened bills staring at me like
neglected kittens imploring their mother for food. I have no food nor
any more patience with this dogged year. and then this: a book reviewer
said the other day I was not a "real writer." ha, a
critic I'd like to present with a Brooklyn cheer. uh-huh,
my idea of a homemade Kwanzaa gift. but,
ah me, I am content to shadow-box with jesus, like the wu-tang's ghostface

killah. indeed, I am so hip-hopped out I may proclaim the
Beatles more vital than jesus and dare any pop-master cuttin and
scratchin historical fables
to prove a party in the boogie down bronx, circa 1983, is more liberating
than my Toshiba, circa the new millennium—

Sunday, December 31, 2000
11:34AM

KEVIN POWELL

Incense—lit

blue

lavery   s
catching the trane
cres   a
4   0
tenor
for dinner
kinda
like his mind a
thelonius crossed-foot slide
broom strokes run parallel with the ankle
avery   sl
a rolling stone terrible & strange saga
de tupac amaru
de sabah as sabah
conmigo   hoppin' john
or rice and peas
neither
please
just an intruder (or 2) in my crib
they took my milk bottle and towed my bed down dekalb avenue past spike's
joint
& the brooklyn hospital
they were on top of me crying that they was dying
they crucified my sleep and made room for themselves
down by my pig guts
& the watermelon & the goobers
they jackhammered chains to my
funk
like august wilson
say: true dat!
i'ma be a big man—
and they smokes the room...igh
h:

1996

Will those dreams
I had as a child come
to pass Will I fall
through the sky
landing in a pit
of purple rats as
the apocalypse
loosens its belt
and beats the
pavement until
welts the size of
africa's left nostril
quakes my puny
bones leaving
me levitating
in pork as I
scramble beneath
my folding bed the
darkness so prison-like
that even my mother
southern warrior
that she is cannot
scrape the tinted
windows off that
child's imagination Will
I die the day that I am
born the gunshot residue
of my mother's two failed
abortions black boy richard
wright detested himself
and me twin negroes
who dream too damn
much about death 'cept
we a living death and
a living lie because ma
said the truth shall set
you free and a lie will

WHAT THE DEAL, SON?
WHAT THE DEAL, SON?

leave you dead as the
bleached lips mister littlejohn
would brush with
the stories snared between
his gangrene tongue and that vaseline
they call bacardi I had a dream
about old man littlejohn
and his bacardi dreamt
he was trying to set
the world on fire and ain't
had no matches so he
poured that bacardi all
over his body until
him smelled like baby
powder with a 72-year-
old butt infection and
well Will you understand
when I say mister
littlejohn died the day
he recognized his back
had been a throw rug
longer than it took that
bacardi to burn the corns
from his feet he dead
dead like a ghetto baby
slurping the dust from
his crack mother's nipples
dead dead like the drug
dealer harvesting crops
on this concrete plantation
dead dead like the black
leader whose chicken-greased
oratory sounds like the slave
master's booted foot caving
in my skull dead dead as I felt
in church every Sunday
as reverend right on
stretched forth his mighty
pockets and emptied hell

into my lap its fiery flesh
heated like a jigga who
thought this kiss of the
glass straw would be the one
to put him in orbit without
the space shuttle bringing
him nearer god to me
bow-legged black boy
who became an insomniac
as a man so terrified of sleeping
'cause, like nas said, sleep
is the cousin of death 'cept
death ain't got no cousins
so sleep must be death
and dreaming must be
god usurping salvador
dalí's juice and bypassing
the most fundamental
question of a dreamer Will
you mind if I tell you I
believe in god but it
just might not be the
god you believe in

Saturday, August 21, 1999
12:45AM

KEVIN POWELL

WHAT THE DEAL, SON?

What the deal, son?

The Soul of Summertime

Just when things seem to be gettin' worse around the way—*so-and-so got shot, that girl's havin' another baby, homeboy's pops got the AIDS*—summer in all its multiflavored blissfulness steps to us, bathes us in sunshine, and says, Yo, kid, everything's gonna be aiight.

Really, though, there is something truly therapeutic, even liberating, about the sights, sounds, and soul of summer: the boys scopin' out the girls and the girls scopin' out the boys, the colorful and all-too-revealing clothes, the mobile stereo systems better known as cars and jeeps, the all-day barbeques and spirited games of dominoes, the tiny bodies splashing through water blasting from open hydrants, and all the folks taking in the show from the safety of their rooftops and fire escapes.

Summertime is like that cool-ass cousin from down South who makes his or her way to the big city just to chill for a few months and—along the way—shows you things you never dreamed possible: walks in the park with a newfound love, house parties without beefs or turf wars, music festivals where your body moves in ways your mama said would surely lead you to the Devil, and a scorching sun that makes it okay to sweat and smell a little funky 'cause *everybody* is sweaty and funky.

That cool-ass cousin knows what time it is: time to lay back in the cut, reflect, regroup from a hellish winter or a hard year at school, switch jobs, plot for the rest of the year, and eat as much food as you can—especially when somebody else is cooking it.

And just like that cool-ass cousin when he or she's about to peace you out and head home, as summer fades, you can't help but smile and say, *Thanks for everything. I can't wait to see you again next year.*

June 1996

Reality Check
For Kurt Cobain (1967 - 1994)

K
E
V
I
N

P
O
W
E
L
L

i hate myself and want to die
i can hear you saying that now
the words like gunshots blasted into
the skin silencing the nightmares of a
generation we are not an x or twenty-
something
there is more to our teen spirit
it smells like distorted childhoods
and diapered friendships and parents
who fed us watergate and vietnam
and ronald reagan and saturday morning
cartoons without giving us a love we could
grip and suck on when the earth
was burning in our direction
and now you are gone
nah! i refuse to believe that
a whole bunch of us were gonna go and listen to you
regurgitate our blues (yours too) and make anxiety-filled
guitar licks into a futuristic rock opera (our opera)
your hair would fly like a stringy flag saluting the knuckleheads of
the world, yes! us! the post-civil rights post-vietnam post-reagan
babies would somehow feel validated when your hoarse, garbled
tongue slapped the world with an indictment that said "you have
neglected us for too long and look, just look at what you have created"
and we would mosh and slam-dance, our bodies contaminated with
this thing called youth, into a fitful overdose (isn't that what they expect of
us anyhow?) of icon-worshipping you: but you are
alive!
tongue-kissing your feminine side on saturday night live
alive!
eating environmentally sound fruit next to river phoenix
and you whisper in james dean's ear
as janis, jimi, jim and john, the post-
happy days mount rushmore,
fall stone in love with the grunge thing
and someone will fanzine you
and call you a tragic genius
and bury you in mtv heaven
because no one no one no one
will ever understand why your flannel shirts
and ripped jeans and busted guitars mean

you have loved and lived much longer
than most of us....

1994

REALITY
CHECK
REALITY CHECK

Street Vendor

ahma be rich one day—you wait and see
man shoot, ahm tired of bein poor
tired of sellin these incense and these oils
been workin too hard, you know?
use to own my own business, couple of 'em, matter of fact
maybe ah just didn't have the right formula though
swore ah'd be rich by now
but ahm gonna make that million, you watch—
either ahm gonna be rich or ahm gonna be dead....

Sunday, April 14, 1996

(Y)our mouth(s)

i'll be straightforward. happy
to receive your postmark 8/7, dated 7/30.
high top fades should converse. atlanta
eyes like hawks troopin' through a sewer
a moment, really, to plant and germinate
the harlem renaissance the black arts move
meant new voices old voices post-integration
blues kids but bomkauf isneverwas an
asterisk on my sole try earlyjonesginsbergkerouac
i dance nude on the front porch hiding is for
literaryfascists sippin' glue in academia
praytell what is a poem is poetry if it is not
a ballooned version of one's hairy butt cheeks?
ink is derivative (mine, i.e.) of hiphop standing
on the verge of a drumbeat the noise scares me
to death a special focus is tangible though
just shake the barbed wire from yo mouth.

1992

come sunday
this god that goddess
and these ancestors
will knock the earth upside down
and loose the devil from his space shuttle
pop a hole in the boy in the plastic bubble
and dream a heaven
where we won't have to wait until
the other side of yesterday
to open our judgment letters

lawd knows we ain't done nothin' that bad
to be *this* black and blue
lawd knows that these black, brown, and beige feet
done seen a lot of sundays come and go
lawd knows sunday is the day when
these black, brown, and beige feet
compete
with that death bell banging its head
against the squeals of a new-born baby

come sunday
what will we call this new-born baby?
let us call him ra—god of the sun
let us call her isis—mother of creation and the universe
let us baptize this new-born baby with a red
thunderbolt from shango

come sunday
let us remember this new-born baby when he
becomes tommy, a harlem hiphopper whose tongue
is an orange-brown razor blade
whose soul is the heated piss on the potholed slab
of st. nicholas avenue

come sunday
let us praise this b-boy
this drug dealer turned junkie
this god-child who is parked, trembling, at an

intersection, eating a chocolate hostess cupcake
the sugar jutting from his wrists
the way blood spewed from jesus' in that picture

come sunday let us remember
what someone's grandmother murmured to us:

that that boy they call jesus gonna creep
back like a thief in the night
and he might just be a junkie
with a bottle of liquor
nailed to *his* fingers….

come sunday
we will look in the mirror and hear venus
bathing that junkie between her legs:
the sugar, the blood, the love
resurrecting the armageddon we missed the
first time

come sunday
we will not ask who that is
who is so unashamed of their nakedness?
come sunday
we will mount duke ellington's piano
plunk syllables from nina simone's microphone
trail john coltrane to a pentacostal retreat
memorize aretha franklin's prescriptions for the soul
and, this time, listen to the smoking gun in tupac shakur's eyes

come sunday
come sunday
come sunday
we will not ask who that is
because we will know
that in the church
in the mosque
at the shrines
near the altars

inside those roots
behind the wax dripping from that white candle
there is a god
there is a goddess
there is a power
this sunday
that sunday
every sunday
because every day is sunday
and one day
it will come to pass
that the god, the goddess
we've been looking for
has been here all along
right over here near our frozen footsteps
and our rubber soles…
come sunday
come sunday
come sunday
come sunday—

July 1998

come sunday |

NO!

for Aishah Shahidah Simmons*

Will us boys ever learn that power
can't be pulled from the meat of our third leg
like the last taste of malt liquor sucked from the
bottom of a bottle? Will we ever cease to find
our torsos slow-dragging with death, our dance
a series of grenades aimed at the bellies of our
mothers' daughters? Will us boys ever break ranks
with the devil, his bible telling us it is mad cool
to rape women because the master does it, and
don't we, too, yearn to be masters? Will we ever
be able to glue back the hair, unswell the eye,
dab away the blood, and stitch up the holes of the women
we have knifed, repeatedly, with our hatred and
fear? Will us boys ever be able to admit that
some of us have become predators, our prey the
neighbor, the girlfriend, the wife, the sister,
the niece, the granddaughter whose life is an
unguarded prison cell loaded with screams,
paranoia, and a body unsure why it now eats itself?

Friday, December 31, 1999

*Aishah Shahidah Simmons is a rape survivor and the writer, director, and producer of *NO!* a documentary about rape and sexual assault.

A Poem Written After Seeing 'Basquiat,' The Movie

dey
eben
cill
us
afta
we
ded

1996

K E V I N   P O W E L L

Southern Birth
For Lottie Bur(r)ison Powell (February 23, 1912 – May 16, 1988)

a procession. southern wails. a yellow
face emerges specked with black moles.
two pennies slit the eyes where the dirt road
used to be. those thick glasses
distract from the tobacco-stained
teeth. tingling carolina stench braid
coarse charcoal hair.

i ache until it is wet, naked,
full of bounce: a gushing wind
corners a heart; puffy cotton veins
snap the way grandma lottie
broke string beans in the front yard.
a moist sound spills onto
the dirty plywood. reverend wilson's
eulogy fogs the church. homemade
syrup and cornbread descend. my mouth
plummets into an emotional abyss: a lover
flees the outhouse and a baby inherits the pain.

1993

Where Brooklyn At

After Langston Hughes

Where do we go after
we
die
is it
to hell
to smell
the devil's fish fry
or
is it
to heaven
to catch
the lord
in
a
lie
?

Where do we go after
we
die
is it
to the grave
where slaves
wear platinum
chains
or
is it
to the ocean
where
washed-out ghosts
stake their claims
?

Where do we go after
we
dle
is it

to the liquor store
to spill dust
for the others who ain't here
or
is it
to the freezer
to eat
the meat
that has disappeared
?

Thursday, January 25, 2001

inside those roots
behind the wax dripping from that white candle
there is a god
there is a goddess
there is a power
this sunday
that sunday
every sunday
because every day is sunday
and one day
it will come to pass
that the god, the goddess
we've been looking for
has been here all along
right over here near our frozen footsteps
and our rubber soles…
come sunday
come sunday
come sunday
come sunday—

July 1998

K E V I N   P O W E L L

come sunday |

NO!

for Aishah Shahidah Simmons*

Will us boys ever learn that power
can't be pulled from the meat of our third leg
like the last taste of malt liquor sucked from the
bottom of a bottle? Will we ever cease to find
our torsos slow-dragging with death, our dance
a series of grenades aimed at the bellies of our
mothers' daughters? Will us boys ever break ranks
with the devil, his bible telling us it is mad cool
to rape women because the master does it, and
don't we, too, yearn to be masters? Will we ever
be able to glue back the hair, unswell the eye,
dab away the blood, and stitch up the holes of the women
we have knifed, repeatedly, with our hatred and
fear? Will us boys ever be able to admit that
some of us have become predators, our prey the
neighbor, the girlfriend, the wife, the sister,
the niece, the granddaughter whose life is an
unguarded prison cell loaded with screams,
paranoia, and a body unsure why it now eats itself?

Friday, December 31, 1999

*Aishah Shahidah Simmons is a rape survivor and the writer, director, and producer of *NO!* a documentary about rape and sexual assault.

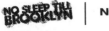

altar for four
inspired by the art of Radcliffe Bailey

I.

four little girls

    bombed for equal rights
a prayer yes yes say a prayer, brother
for the forgotten
      we
         shall
              overcome
our overcomes and our overcames

DEAD

four little black girls

bodies greased, pressed and folded against the church pews
their heads
like halos
glow beneath the lord's window
no, sister
that window is not there anymore
it exploded on four little girls
the way that water hose broke old mister young's back
oh people, can you hear me?
        what do we want?
    freedom!
        when do we want it?
    now!
thirty years and counting
been countin' for thirty years now
done run out of toes and fingers to count on

II.

    john coltrane
        where have you gone?
we can still feel your sax dragging its tongue

 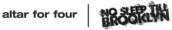

along the carpet they call alabama
          sweet sweet alabama
land of the cotton
          why are those four little black girls
still bleeding in your belly?

III.

brothas and sistas, hah!
i'm here ta tell ya, hah!
that the laaawd don't like ugly, no! lawd don't like no ugliness
are y'all wid me?
i said are y'all wid me now?
these little girls ain't done nothin' to noooo-body
i said noooo-body
and for that they dead lawd
look at them sweet jeee-sus!
ain't got no toes left, hah!
ain't got no fingers left, hah!
can't count the time no more lawd, hah!
time done stop lawd, hah!
i said time done stop, hah!
what we gonna do lawd?
we gonna pick some flowers, hah!
and bury our future, hah!
and we gonna build a new house lawd
and we gonna paint it blue lawd
i said we gonna paint it blue, hah!
so we can feel that old-time spirit a-goin', hah!
feeel it! thank ya jesus!
feeel it! thank ya jesus!

IV.

at 16th and 6th they say it's
          not a home anymore
they say all the homes have been torn down
          that blackfolks don't live here anymore

just dusty flesh and charcoal bones
        with steam-iron memories
of this march or that song
they say
        the railroad tracks have moved
that just because you can cross 'em now
don't mean you gotta new home
you still gotta pack a gun
still gotta poke it into the sky like this:
bang!
they say:
        we're not bitter
            just hungry
                need some nourishment
                and some time
                and some homes
                                and some freedom...

1993

Postblack

how
can
we
b
post
black
when
they
act
like
we
r
not
even
post
colored?

Sunday, November 18, 2001
7:33PM

Trees on our backs
inspired by a series of "Beloved"-related paintings by Renaldo Davidson

They done paralyzed our tongues with vinegar and a garlic noose
    swept the men away with a fractured mirror and a half-broom
    bolted the women to the cargo criss-crossing their bosoms
    buried the children alive in the feces of a dead dream
    kidnapped that old preacher and bid her to cast her gut
        in the 'cane field
    canceled our mass therapy session and told us not to dance no more
    inhabited our hands, urging us to slit the souls of our kinfolk
    sponged the life from our bodies and watched us confront the sun
        for more time
    painted the earth red and laughed as we vomited the blood
        spraying from our rubbery limbs
    soaked us in the atlantic, then dried us with a mule whip—

We say:

They done put trees on our backs.

Thursday, December 24, 1998
12:14AM

darryl strawberry fields forever

the new york times magazine
called you "an american tragedy"
but i say what do they know
of tragedies if they refuse, even now,
to consider slavery, that long-running
catastrophe this nation was built upon?
indeed, when did slavery end, really, darryl?
when did the lash cease to
sting, the noose cease to hang,
the dreams cease to be death, shivering,
hunched over, and huddled between
the cocaine lines of the lord's prayer?
or did we simply drift from
the plantations to the factories to
the ballfields to the crackhouses—
a succession of toxic spaces for the colored
orphans, stone cold in love with
america? and the colored orphans yowl, sheepishly,
where have you gone darryl strawberry—
a nation grimaces and turns its guilty eyes
away from you: your body, formerly mud-brown
and as buffed as a new slave ripped from
africa's ass is now splintered like the baseball
bats you once gripped: say, today, you don't have your
hands on the gun-barrel, darryl. say it ain't so—

Saturday, April 6, 2002
8:22PM

Blues for Charlie

for Charlie Braxton

What does death look like, Charlie?
How does it feel to know that
You are still regarded as a slave
As a bent-back, toothless Mississippi sharecropper
Three-fifths of a human being
A second-class citizen
Invisible
As you laid in that bed
The smoke and fire's sandpapered arms
Eager to transport you
Broken feet first
To that nappy, unshaven wilderness they call heaven?
Did you see Jesus, Charlie, as you swam frantically
On your back? Or were you watching your life
Stumble and slide across the creaky
Floorboards like a freshly poisoned
Ghetto rat?
What does death taste like, Charlie?
Is it the flavor of Emmitt Till's vomit
Snapping a whistling boy's neck?
Or is it the morbid aftertaste of crooked
Po-lice and emotionally detached firemen filing
Their fingernails as *your* nails burrow into the bed sheets?
Does anyone see your bed sheets—your makeshift coffin—
Bleeding the tears of a man left for dead? Wasn't that man
They called Medgar Evers a good man, and left, dead? Would
We have asked if you were a good man? Would we have left,
You, dead, had it not been for your wife? Does anyone
Know that colored women got hearts made of pure
African diamonds? That those diamonds have cut the
Fat from the hate in the world and boiled the leftover
Meat 'til love done burnt our one good pot? Did anyone
See your wife hurtle through Mississippi's constipated history
Bringing you from the fields to the city and back again? Did anyone
See, Charlie, that death don't look like you?

Sunday, April 28, 2002
11:41PM

KEVIN POWELL

Blues for Charlie

37

(self)portrait (the remix)

i was born a year after Malcolm was blown away, two years before a rifle stifled MLK, and five years before Tupac would step, flippin' the bird, onto the stage. i am the only child of a young single Geechee woman who grey-hounded it from a shotgun shack to a northern tenement. city slicker raised with a southern sensibility: that means i like ketchup on my scrambled eggs, hot sauce on my grits, and i don't sing before the mornings out 'cuz i don't want to be mad the rest of the day. means, as ma said, if you make your bed hard you gonna sleep in it hard, fuh shizzle. i've wanted to be a writer since i was a shorty of 11. ma-dukes took me to the greenville public library in jersey city, new jersey—where i was pimp-smacked into life—most saturdays. i overdosed on music, tv, sports, Hemingway, Poe, Shakespeare, and so much candy i would see spots with my eyes wide shut. thought my childhood was one long misery session, complete with hunger, violence, and rage. escaped from the concrete box to college on a financial aid package but i have made several trips back to the gutter because there is no safety net for field negroes with rebellion on they brain. no matter, adolescent dream fulfilled: done scrapped together several books and my name done been in *Vibe, Code, Rolling Stone, Newsweek, the Washington Post, Essence, Ms.*, and elsewhere. i rest my head these days on that planet they call brooklyn, new york. don't need to know where brooklyn at 'cuz it in me like africa all up in me, ya smell me? a necessary aside, cousin: i ain't the man i use to be nor the man i want to be either, but i am trying, really am, y'all. cannot obliterate the past and know i have messed up but i ain't a messed up person. all that therapy and spiritual warfare and self-reflecting and conversating, as we say, has worked at least a little miracle, nahmean? aiight, then, the finale: i write 'cuz my moms now asks me to spell and pronounce words for her and 'cuz my maternal grandparents could not read or write. I write 'cuz I wanna be free *before* I die, knowwhatahmsayin'?

Sunday, March 2, 2003
1:38PM

Katrina

Here
I am
My lawd
On top of this roof
Can't nobody hear my cry
I said
Here I am my lawd
On top of this roof
Can't nobody hear my cry
My lawd
I am thirsty
My lawd
I am hungry
My lawd
I am lonely
My lawd
I need your help
Because they keep passing me by
I said I need your help, my lawd
Because they keep passing me by
I did nothing, my lawd
I have nothing, my lawd
I need something, my lawd
Because Ka-tri-na—
Done broken the levee
Ka-tri-na—
Done made my load heavy
Ka-tri-na—
Done made me ready
For that long walk to you
Ka-tri-na—
Done made me ready
For that long talk with you
My lawd
I am coming—
To get my due
My lawd

I am coming—
To cash my check
Here I am, my lawd
Here
I am—

Thursday, November 17, 2005
12:30PM

Part II. love/a many splintered thing

NO SLEEP TILL BROOKLYN

love/a many splintered thing

for Karla P.

i have this need to feel you
make love out of the sweat
itching our palms give
you to your mother so that she
can give birth to you create an
ocean where love sleeps peacefully
eat out of the same bed we flesh
orgasms scream where cobwebs
imprison courage cry where
your tears gripped my shoulders wrap
my tongue around your waist and
lick the rhythms of your walk
talk until a beat hits me where
it hits me where it hits me
in the space   where my heart
used to be   you know it's
blank now   dark   black no
commercials open land
waiting to be folded and smoothed
out like the note i slipped you yesterday
that said you are me am you we are
do not be afraid i want to
help you help me   love a
many splintered thing i felt
yes   his tongue slit my heart
as it parted your mouth
and i wanted to die yeah
rope myself with my naiveté
drink reflection: share a walk on
lenox avenue with a friend who
gets high on pain   two many times
we step on our eyelids and miss
the chance to l(i)ove   the chance
to slide open a cloud with a kiss
when will trust not be for sale   a
gun between the thighs a middle
finger aimed at the hungry   a wish
stuffed inside two bodies crawling
on their tails scraping the bottom
of a dream

1992

Not for Nothing

I cannot erase all the women I've been with
nor can I firebomb the past and bang the ashes into my grandmother's land
but I do understand
when you say
'Men are just that way'
I do not want to be 'that way'—
after tonight I feel as if
I could churn love from your muscled thighs
cop diamonds from your brown-button nipples
eat dessert
where god (her)
told the ancestors (them)
there is loneliness east of eden—
east of you is a player who
craves a tomboy with shin splints and a blood-red
chest: is that your heart, cut like a tomato, squirting
me in the eyes from behind your iron gate?
east of you is a player who
wants to atomic-bomb that gate
crawl to your bedroom roll my tongue
along the leather lining of your stomach
comb your short, metallic hair with my teeth
and, not for nothing, kiss your lips until they
overflow like the mississippi

Sunday, April 1, 2001
3:04PM

KEVIN POWELL

April in Brooklyn

for Danielle

I can still smell you in my bed/
it is the smell of california palm trees
peppery louisiana gumbo
and a sweaty medicine-woman slinging
the mudcake from her dimpled walls(
I am at a stage in my life where a
hug is as crucial as the air backing into my throat)
that we hold each other so easily says to me loneliness
is like blowing scar tissue into that steel beam we christened
april. april is the month my moms led a
ferocious slave revolt and named me a seam,
a pulse, a child of the monkey, half of the ibeyi (but
where might my other half be, my sister?(i know
I may never be you again so I say 'thank-you'
for loaning me your marrow and your bones last night. and, no,
I do not see you simply as a sex object. indeed,
I would like to delete that digital photograph
and start anew: forgive me, friend-in-the-making,
that my (self-)love is jacked up like memories
of the master separating us at death and commanding
us to bop, like bojangles, until our feet are
a ragged blue like the sky this month in bruk-nam. it
does not matter, you, if the reader knows
not of bruk-nam; we do, and if I never
never stroke you there again, never
never eat with you again,
know that april would have been the cruellest
month without the goddess we call your cat-heat.

Saturday, April 21, 2001
1:34AM

APRIL IN BROOKLYN

APRIL IN BROOKLYN

APRIL IN BROOKLYN

APRIL IN BROOKLYN

for Danielle

If I could construct the perfect soulmate it would be *you*—

How else am I to begin this sugar-crusted poem about
a love I never expected
a heart palpitation I never detected
a dream I thought would never fade away?
or, more exactly, have I told you
that the very moment
I spotted you, behind the scenes of that show,
that your nile river smile ruptured
the rotting stitches in my mind
and begat a willowy cinnamon
woman I had caressed in another time
in the bush
on that ship called jesus
beyond the earsplitting silence of the middle passage
in the sadistic alleyways of that plantation
at them crossroads
between jim crow and we free—
I say all of this to say
that that night you stood before me
—Saturday, April 7, 2001—
time took off its watch and smashed it to the ground
and I knew, simply, that I needed to know you
that our spirits had once kissed the sky in unison
and that we had traveled from a planet
they call memory to this moment—
and I saw no one else in that universoul
        except you

Tuesday, January 6, 2004
1:06AM

K
E
V
I
N

P
O
W
E
L
L

Fear

Perhaps you thought
me a man in your other life.
But in this one I am the homeboy
who has cemented his feet with the
ice bucket. What is that? you ask.
I reply: It is the dread of scrubbing
the charcoal guts from my doorknob which
makes me so melancholy. Mine
is a spaceless emotion, my baldness
illuminated by the flicker of your lips.
Yet I decline to notarize your lips because,
in so doing, I notarize you and I, and that,
my love, is the weight of *la amistad*
mashing the night as cinque slashes a falling star.
Like *that* weight, I do want our love to be heavy,
and fearless, like a quilt sewed by the chubby,
sausagelike digits of a grandmother. Branded
into that quilt is us, my left hand braided into
your right hand as we vault from the back
of one alligator to another, our ecstasy framed by
the margins of the universe. But if I should rush
from the waterfalls, would you push the
vines from my heart and lug it to
the other side of the quilt?

Monday, January 12, 1998
5:44PM

Love

Love, why are you a red rose
sitting there in a discarded Coca-Cola
bottle atop my coffee table? Do you know
no shame? Are you not worried that some medieval
prophet will hoist you from that bottle, pound your
ruby petals, and pass you to the whirlwind that is emotion?
Does not the whirlwind's caddiness trouble you, love?
Or are you, like me, a hard-headed rose
wistfully awaiting the sun? Perchance you might be stalling
that moment when the sun's hotness will bite
your stem with its yellow teeth, making you
blaze with the passion of a boy
gauging his life by the span of that first
school-yard kiss? Are you, love, the sun-kiss I have
been fiending for since that day?

Monday, May 31, 1999
10:42PM

Vespers
inspired by the film version of "Midnight In The Garden of Good and Evil"

Black. It is black, the day. And I notice that you are on your
heels removing the curls from your hair. In the bathroom, as I read
the expanded art and leisure section of the paper. Sunday's

the day we discuss good and evil, the ways of southern folks, and we
tend to your garden. The garden which is not good, which is not evil,
which is. It is the garden that I prayed in once, in a dream too foggy to

forget. In this dream I was not on my heels, nor my knees. I prayed on my toes in
the middle of an abandoned chimney (there was no house attached to the
chimney) while you played the violin. "Summertime." You played

"Summertime" but it was winter and I thought that an odd selection. "Don't
matter," you said as your chin screwed itself into your violin. "Don't matter 'cuz
nobody can feel it 'cept you." Then you smiled and a notion

engraved a triangle on my left eyeball and made the eyeball jump:

if we cut one of your hair strands in the garden, plant it in the garden's right hip,
then walk seven times over that hip, we—you and I—will hear voices, worn
voices, wailing in the winter chill. And we would gently

seat ourselves in the laps of those voices, fasten our seatbelts, and fly. Past the
demon in the white robe, past the angel in the blue platform shoes, past the
red cat chasing the liquor bottle down the avenue. Past, alas, our mothers'

blunted tree houses.

Into the neglected appendages of midnight.

Tuesday, December 9, 1997
10:14AM

That Thing

I felt uncomfortable watching that movie with you this evening,
knowing that my love has been as stable as a raging hurricane—
Why does maleness so often mean an inability to wear the emotional
dress women don so easily? Are our souls that parched, that we cannot
offer a saliva drop to the women who would simply request "Can you
quench *my* thirst? Can you hold *me*?"? I have no answer for you, because the
nos I've given you have become as foul as dead bodies trapped inside an
empty chamber for months: pesky blind rodents chew those dead bodies, the
stench akin to that thing that rings the heart of a woman who has feigned mental
orgasms far too long. "This is a movie about men who don't know
how to love women," you say, and my body spumes guilt bubbles, the fingers of
my hands puncturing, like darts, each colorless balloon rising from my
cheekbones. "Are you not sympathetic with any of the male characters?" I ask,
stupidly, and you give me that look, as if to say "Are you mad? Why, my heart is
as defeated as that woman's sex drive, and I, too, have felt the pangs of a man's
boomerang." Ah, not the boomerang. Is that what this is about? My love has
been like a boomerang, flung to you, but winding up in my paws, always—Am I
that character who records himself dominating the ocean while he swims, in his
white tee shirt and Gap khakis, on concrete? Am I that character who bends his
lover like a Barbie doll, his pillow monologue the
grenades and sandbags which wedge between her legs? Or am I that character
who spends too much time making love to his own scent, and does not
smell the disappearance of his lover, even after she is gone?

Monday, September 7, 1998
11:59PM

KEVIN POWELL

possibilities

i see you: dancing like a revelation
from an ancestor: chains swing wildly
from your kneecaps; your arms, guideposts
to the yesteryear when you traveled in search of a
beat, hold firm against the hurricanes of time: your
eyebrows, heavy reminders that your momma and your
granny and your great nana pirouetted across your face,
their ankles the ankles of that captured woman spinning
her body into an ocean full of sharks; their ankles the ankles
of a field hand spitting her bastard child into the earth as her
legs, once bent back behind her ears and pinned to the wooden floor,
cry "mercy oh lawd have mercy"; their ankles the ankles of fleeing dancers—
smokey black, rusty brown, redbone, good hair bad hair don't
know what it wanna be hair—their tough, tight, deliberate routine scored by
the bottom of shoes scraping railroad platforms: they migrate their
souls to the top of the promised land, levitating, arms waving
frantically, fingers promising to write that letter, legs escaping them
ropes and them fires and them mean people down the road, over
there yes over there they dance in chicago in new york in detroit in
los angeles in d.c. they toedance, the big toe pointing outward toward
that star, the one that scorched an earth for katherine and carmen and
judith and debbie and you yes they you they you they—you dance a sweetly
chocolate release for the millennium, they see you even when you stop
out of embarrassment they see you and they smile, the footprints
on their crimson colored gums your ticket to fly....

1996

the changes i've been going through
u kiss me that first time it shook
like a d.c. go-go dancer ancient   yes
the emotion rolled back its sleeves
and dipped a man-child's pulse into
u i want(ed) to make love until sperm
& heat & u & me could reconcile our youth
the age of innocence manipulates youme   but
u live with him i liked her   and we kissed:
bodies undressing angerpainconfusion mary j.
blige moaning in the background 'bout two
only children playing with toys toying with
art & adulthood and we framed each other a
mirror skinned it really naked we finger &
nibble & lick   the dust off our loveand
we came   so easily   together to conclude that
this was suppose to be about friendship & not
love-making (evenifitdoesfeelliketheendofthe
worldandweareconnectedonafutondoingasixty-
nineyouowingmeowingyouanothertaste) unless it
means masturbating our souls coaxing a woman
& a man out of that pool of wetness

1992

KEVIN POWELL

anniversary

May I take your tongue and shave it,
backwards, until the pulp has evaporated into my gums?
That is what your love means to me:
that we have the supernatural on our rooftop, its zeal the
color of a rain singeing that dent where the clock once
preached, mocking Lucifer's time. But no more, for we have
done it—we have freed our hearts from those plastic
bags; and those hearts now have the wings we longed
for—wings the breadth of a dream schemed by two babies
bouncing in a pen until their teeth chime, like Carolina sea bells,
at the sight of a black cat's hungry meow.

Thursday, February 12, 1998
12:57AM

To Be Continued

I once stood naked before the devil with piece of a fig leaf
Piercing my left earlobe. If I were not so menaced
Perhaps I really could find the magic in the tragedy of
My tortured life. Yea, I would give anything to be
Born in a time when slavery was not my addiction
To ESPN nor my need, as an artist, to have chaos
In order to make art smell. Did not Baraka say art
Is suppose to beautify the world? Why then, I ask
You, does my art reek of shark-mangled torsos, of
Pissed-on cotton patches, of brown necks and other
Body parts basted with pickle juice like pigs feet and pigs
Knuckles? Does anyone care that history is an email
Being re-routed from my iBook to that federal
Building? Okay, we are a comely people, here—here
Loneliness is defined by instant messages and
Midtown massage parlors where petite Korean women
With burgundy nails pick at my childhood scabs,
Flicking dead, brittle skin to that black-tar playground:
There I swore my moms thought nakedness
A sin while I caught nakedness in a balled up
Paper bag—if only I could find that balled up paper bag....

Sunday, February 4, 2001
1:08AM

KEVIN POWELL

Haiku #2

Yes, I need music.
The rhythms transcend my blues.
Why take that from me?

1991

Oh Love, Oh Where's My Love

There you are,
there:
in God's hand glass,
a holy being
suspended outside my Harlem window
as time and my heartbeat,
fleeing the antagonists' torches,
shutter our eyes, hook arms, and funnel
the currents guiding your hips
along st. nicholas avenue.

Wednesday, December 10, 1997
6:42PM

KEVIN POWELL

OH LOVE,
OH WHERE'S MY LOVE

Oh Love, Oh Where's My Love

55

Of Your Birthday

ma told me, today, "don't let her slip through your fingers";
told ma that ain't gonna happen 'cuz the
Venus's-flytrap is there, between the thumbs and index fingers,
catching you—that part of you which circles our PCs, glides across
the ceiling fan, studies the bloated closet, and delicately
lays itself on the bed on its side, careful not to snap its wings, or slam
its pencil-like finger, again, beneath the windowpane—

that it is your birthday I have not forgotten. that it is the day on which
god dug you from your mother's earth, discharged dirt into your ears
and bade you to be, I have not forgotten either. what I have forgotten, in
the midst of fretting because someone has stolen my pockets, is that love
doesn't need pockets to hold itself, if love's hands and arms are there,
bear-hugging the wind, not embarrassed to admit that its wisdom teeth are
rotten, that it has bad feet, a double chin, or a stomach struggling to peek over
its belt. No, I have never felt like this: like her birthday is my birthday; that is,
that we have carried each other, now, for six months, through the body aches, the
baby kicks inside the heart, the water breaking and flooding our eye patches; and
in spite of the past, its derby pulled down tightly upon its head, its off-white
trenchcoat, wrinkled, soiled, covering the body fat accumulated from years of
neglect—oh how the past nearly caused a miscarriage! oh how the past wrestled
love to the asphalt and demanded love to bow down! and die—

but it is your birthday and you, lioness that you are, roar with the fervor
of a woman possessed by the banshee they could not chain to a pole, or
lash from behind, or dangle from a tree. No! the poltergeist which envelops
your tupac-like eyebrows, your bushy mane, your javelin legs, is the one who
knows she really does not need a birthday because every day, as she rubs moon
droplets from her eyes, she brings forth the snaky crack in the sky we call dawn.

Wednesday, July 30, 1997

And then we kissed

in an italian restaurant
west village mirage—
two mirrors bat eyes
as the piano breaks for a violin concerto—
the food it is good and rich and its oils
balm our lips
lips that have tangoed these two weeks
lips that have been infected by the lotus-eaters
moistened, puffy lips that are brimming with fear and hope and
longing
for the day when we can punish our eggshells
from within
allow the moon to mark our bodies
with abbey lincoln's afro-blue palms
palms safeguarding the yard
where a witch finger-popped the moon,
its blood the baptism
for two gypsies coming home

Monday, March 3, 1997

AND THEN WE KISSED KISSED WE THEN AND

An American Beauty

for M.E.

It is a pity to live amongst the soiled ruins of a fascist,
Don't you think?
I concur with Lester Burnham: It would be beautiful
To be asked, say, 'How are you today?' But, shorty, that
Gesture would be like your boss presently discovering
She has the capacity to milk roses from her breasts
And we know she cannot do that for she does not
Even like the roses He has given you tomorrow.
'I love him' you say and I poke my broken index finger
Into your breath and measure the density of
Your words; how thick and impenetrable the letters
Are that daub hieroglyphic feet at the corners of your
Mouth. He is in love with you, you tell me, and
I am not in disbelief, for I saw the devil's advocate
Drop that ballandchain into his livingroom: He is
A prisoner of tradition and religious guilt. He is
A married man living a single man's nightmare. He
Is Lester's left hand gripping self-love by its collar,
Forcing that collar to pop a red Pontiac Firebird.
Is not life grand when one realizes one should do
What makes one happy, not what one thinks will
make the unhappy happy? Indeed, will the unhappy
Ever be happy when they do not know the beauty
Of their unhappiness? Or, the ugliness that makes
Happiness possible? Enough, you scream, and I
Roll another joint for Lester, his death as inevitable
As your emotional lover's there in front of that
TV set. Does he not see the television shooting
him at the mall yesterday?

Saturday, October 23, 1999
3:00AM

A Prayer

Dear Lawd,
Ah ain't mean t' do dis Lawd. It wuz uh accident God. But God,
Ah done had de baby now an' it ain't
Nothin' Ah kin do but t' raise it.
But God, how cum dat damn C_____ done disown his chile?
Oooh Jee-zus! He 13 years older dan me an' he should know bedder.
Lawd, Ah swear, if Ah known dat he was gonna do dat,
T' me, t' leeve me an' dis chile
Ah sho wouldn't had never let him touch me.
Ahm ashame Lawd 'cause dis baby ain't got no daddy.
Ah donno know where t' turn. Ah kin't go back down South
'Cause dey'll call me a *heffa*.
Oh God! *Pleeze* show me de way 'cause dis
Ain't gonna be eazy.
All Ah ask Lawd is dat you give me de strenth
T' take care of dis chile 'til he grown
Enuf t' do fo' hisself.
An' Lawd, when dat boy gits t' be uh man-size, if he ever run int'
His daddy, let him make his daddy pay fo' what he done did.
Ahm sorry, Lawd, fo' sayin' it lak dat but dat's de way Ah feel God.

Ah-man.

1988

KEVIN POWELL

Where's My Daddy?

Ma?
        Yeah boy?
Where's my daddy?
        You ain't got no daddy, boy.
Where did I come from ma?
        You came from me.
But teacher told us that you need a mommy and a daddy to make me.
        What your teacher tellin' you that for?
She said everybody should have a mommy and a daddy.
        Well, your teacher might be right but you ain't got no daddy.
Why ain't I got no daddy ma?
        Because—
Because what?
        Because he wuzn't no good, like most of 'em.
But I want a daddy like everybody else.
        You ain't got one boy, except me—I'm your daddy.
You don't look like no daddy to me.
        Boy, don't you sassy me.
I ain't ma, but where's my daddy?
        I donno boy. Leave me alone.
But ma, where did I come from?
        Ah, you, um, you came from a deer. We went to the woods and kilt a deer
        and made you from it.
For real?
        Uh-huh.
So the deer is my daddy, ma?
        No, you ain't got no daddy.
Why not?
        'Cause.
'Cause what?
        'Cause I said so. Now hush up before I slap you for askin me all
        them fool questions!
I'm sorry ma but I wanna know where's my daddy?

1989

why come?

how
could a man
who knows
so many
people
helps
so many
people
is
so many
people
be
so completely
lonely?

Thursday, May 8, 2003
12:55AM

KEVIN POWELL

Here, take this

Here,
take this,
my heart—
it is picasso's paintbrush
in your hands:
Will me into
technicolors
no bare feet
can smear
golden-haired water
no sponge
can disappear
lost-found objects
no grumpy recycler
can claim
a radcliffe bailey drawing
no canvas
can contain
a brown, bottomless birdcage
we can
hammer to the horizon
a mayan-inspired mural
only your untamed love
can imagine—

**Friday, December 31, 2004
9:08AM**

For You

Today the pressing of my lips against yours
Felt like I was kissing God herself
For you are the shrine of the Black Madonna
I've been waiting to dig up and sanctify
By eating that onion huddled just below the pit of your stomach—
Yes, I hunger for a purposeful love like yours:
Could you tell by the way I fingered your palms
As if there was a volcano inside your hands?
Could you tell by the way I stroked your biceps
As if there was an inferno inside your bosom?
"U were getting me very excited...." you texted me later
And I must confess that I too was taken to a place
Where flesh and blood visit that holy city we call desire
And I imagined us making love with our winter clothes on:
Your mind our opening prayer and foreplay for the babies not yet born
Your body our initiation into the love our mothers' were denied
Your soul our nightdream that this song is but
The beginning of time, a time when this girl and this boy
Will cultivate that woman and that man and
Love each other as if judgement day itself would
Be determined by how hard we make it rain

Saturday, February 10, 2007
10:53PM

KEVIN POWELL

FOR YOU

for aunt cathy

life ain't never been promised to nobody
that's what grandma lottie used to say
and you
her youngest daughter
and youngest of six children
snuck into the city
on a greyhound bus
with my mother
and scraped the side of a boarding house for good luck
as your life stretched beyond
the wooden shacks
and cotton fields
and the sandy school room floors of south carolina

and you were alive
at last
free
in a city
away from the
comforting stench of down south
and in the big city
with its
musty underarm
and gasoline breath

and you took all ten years of your schoolin'
and applied for a job as a factory worker
on the assembly line
and you assembled parts
and the parts assembled you into
the permanence of minimum wages
and time clocks
and bosses who thought a black woman
was supposed to like work
hell, y'all had been conditioned to be oxes
they figured

and when you wasn't producing like an ox
their tucked-in pot bellies would ask:
why you moving so slow cathy?
and on the inside you licked your tongue

at them the way you used to do
when my mother and my aunt birdie yelled at you
and your heart tightened around your waist
and you ate what your feet could produce
for eight hours a day
40 hours a week
with
one 15 minute break a day
if you was doing your job

and you needed something else
to keep your tears from spitting out
thoughts and words that would send you
back down south
in a fit of fear
and you met him
and he was fine
that man
and you liked him
and he liked you
and like became love
to you
and like became lust
for him
and he and you
exploded into anthony
my cousin anthony
one april day in 1966
and now you had a shield
to hold against the world
you had a world to shield you against
the heartaches of him
the foot aches of work
and the headaches
of city life

and you raised anthony
the best way you knew how
just like my mother raised me
and anthony grew and i grew
with our frustrated imaginations
to resent each other
to hate you, our mothers
to despise our very existences

for aunt cathy |

in that tiny
cramped three-room apartment
two mothers and two sons
in a three-room apartment
held together
by welfare
food stamps
and the roaches
who always found their way
into our food
no matter how thick
the layers of aluminum foil

and that thirsty, tingling sensation
would often reappear
crawling between your toes
up your legs
across your thighs
teasing your crotch
but it couldn't get any further
that's nasty,
you thought,
some man between my legs
again
so you stuffed your womb
with the world of anthony
because your spirit
was tired of being probed
by social workers, mailmen, and would-be husbands
for having an illegitimate son

and in spite of reality
burning down every hope we had
we managed to spread out
to a better part of the ghetto
and we even had separate apartments now
but you and my mother
always was in the same building because
my mother was the mean one
who scoffed at the world
with her angry eyes
and you was the nice one
who wanted to be like my mother
but you couldn't

 | **for aunt cathy**

so you followed my mother
everywhere
because at least you'd be safe
from yourself

and when we finally moved out of the ghetto
around white folks
you felt good
we was movin' up
and flying like birds released from their mother's grip for the first time
and we was happy to be around
white folks
and didn't mind being called niggas
because at least we was good niggas

and me and anthony
knocked off the weight of
that restless city
that dirty city
and we left:
me to college
anthony to the navy
leaving you and my mother
grazing in the pastures of mid-life

and my mother was happy to be free of a man-child
but you was sad
because anthony had been your reason to live
your reason to work
your reason to exist
and now his departure meant your death
and you were dying
a slow death
dancing with mid-life and dying a muted death
the years of working were gone
the years of sharing were gone
the years of being were gone
and the woman inside of your crouching body
died one may day in 1988 when grandma lottie was buried
and as we wiped the tears from our eyes
no one noticed you sinking through the church pew
through the floor
into the earth to join grandma lottie

KEVIN POWELL

FOR AUNT CATHY

for aunt cathy |

and even though anthony was there at the funeral
he left again
back to the navy
back to japan
to some strange place
that was not him
because he hated himself
and he hated you
for being him
and he nailed shut
the door
on your life

and no one noticed you drowning in your pain
until you began having conversations with yourself
and tellin' everyone how you was hearing things
and seeing movies on your living room wall
how you was the star in those movies

and even my mother
with her superstitious ways
could not believe
that you were a victim of roots and magic spells

and my mother and aunt birdie did it;
they tricked you with a meal and had you straight-jacketed
and they didn't tell me
but i found out and i found you
and i leaped inside your body
and begged you to wake up
i swam inside your dried up tears
and turned back the currents
to your childhood
to your adolescence
to your early adulthood
to anthony
to anthony's father
to my mother and aunt birdie and grandma lottie
and i cried between the lines of your history

and you told me you were not crazy
and i said i know
and you told me you could not understand
why my mother and aunt birdie had put you there

and i said i know
and you told me how they drugged you
how they called you by a number
how they monitored your phone calls
and i knew that you had become a prisoner of your worst fears
        of your own death

and i looked at you and i didn't see you
instead i saw an old black woman
inside your 45-year-old body
and i wanted to rush to you and shake your youth
out of that impostor

but it was you...

and now i understand those sounds you heard
and those movies you saw on your walls
you are not crazy
it took me a long time
but i understand
anthony knows what you've been through
but he doesn't know you
i know you
my mother and aunt birdie know what you've been through
but they don't know you
i know you

i carry you with me every day
i see you when i see that black woman
lying on the ground with a mcdonald's cup in her hand
at 34th street
i see you and i say
"here cathy,
this is all i got"
and i drop a tear into your cup
and curse myself and my mother and aunt birdie
and anthony and anthony's father
and i kiss you with a prayer
because now i understand
why black bodies sag the way they do
and why black hearts don't birth emotions anymore

1990

for aunt cathy |

Amor

for Danielle

I have never loved a woman the way I love you—
And I regret that I've never had the opportunity,
Fully, to plant chocolate rose petals in your secret garden
To tongue-kiss the earth where your bare feet have crossed
Or to bow down to the majesty of your moonlit gumbo—
I adore you, not until the end of time, but until that
Yesterday when the big bang is our lips burning the past
In that future, a future where our bodies
Will mouth Spanish with our legs intertwined, where Neruda's
Lyrical machete chops up the terrors of our childhoods
Where *amor* is not something we make, not something
We feel, but something we are, for each other, far
Beyond that sun-less crack in the cosmos they call forever—

*Amor means *love* in Spanish

Thursday, July 26, 2007
8:02AM

Jersey City
inspired by Richard Wright

It was at 116 Bergen Avenue, in a cluttered first-floor apartment at the back of the building, that Jersey City, where I was born and where I would spend the first eighteen years of my life, began to disrobe itself, fascinating me, annoying me, and tempting me simultaneously. Each event, each moment, outside and indoors, I held onto tightly, afraid that if I let go, then that event, that moment, would be gone forever:

Like the winded rapture of playing on the black and gray gravel of Audubon Park: climbing the monkey bars, coasting hands-free down the sliding board, or kicking my feet toward the clouds as my mother pushed me on the swings.

Like the instant worldliness rooted in the regular Saturday afternoon rides with my mother on the crowded orange and white Bergen Avenue bus.

Like the longing for adventure induced by the teenage boys who scrambled after a bus, only to grab hold of the back window during a stop, then ride for blocks until the police chased them off—and away.

Like the bewilderment I felt when rain smeared the bright red bricks of 116 Bergen Avenue into a dull, purplish hue.

Like that fleeting taste of nature manifested when my cousin Anthony and I yanked the tiny green leaves from a bush and aimed them at each other's mouths.

Like the experience of death without dying whenever a mutt or an alley cat was struck by a passing car or bus, then lurched and moaned pitifully on the sidewalk before confronting the ground.

Like the peculiar sensation of watching a drunk or junkie tilt toward the earth, only to right himself, piss on himself, curse himself or the nearest neighbor, then march, dignified, down the block.

Like the hostile paranoia I felt whenever my mother and I trekked Jackson Avenue, past the empty, boarded up buildings, past the garbage-strewn lots, past the stink, unshaven men with their pocket-size bottles of liquor.

Like the naive assumption that Jersey City was splitting in half whenever I saw a new crack in the concrete leading to my building.

Like the sugary nostalgia that kissed my eyes whenever I spotted yet another pair of grimy sneakers dangling from the electric wires overhead.

Like the raw titillation discharged when ice cream truck music caromed off my ears onto the ears of Anthony and so on, until all of us ghetto children were spellbound and sprinting, triumphantly, toward the truck.

Like the unsolicited pity of observing pigeons as they battled over a strap of bread.

Like the cryptic sense of great expectations when I angled my head skyward and snared snowflakes on the rim of my bottom lip.

Like the apocalyptic sound of thunder and the mercurial sight of lightning which propelled my mother and Aunt Cathy to snatch off the lights, to unplug all the electrical items, and to forbid Anthony and I from speaking or moving, until that sound and that sight had expended themselves and retired to the heavens.

Like the surge of power I savored when I trapped a cockroach with a plastic top and mocked its maneuvers to free itself.

Like the hot panic which forced its muscular hands around my throat whenever I heard the bustling feet of rats in the walls.

Like the musty air of predictability associated with the white rice my mother served with every dinner.

Like the ungovernable hunger I had whenever my mother baked a thickly crusted sweet potato pie and set it in the refrigerator to cool.

Like the magical appearance of dust rays as the sun's tongue lapped the windows of our apartment.

Like the budding selfishness of my cousin Anthony and I any time we hid our toys from each other.

Like the sudden and inexplicable happiness that rocked me in its strong arms on the occasion of Mister Rogers inviting me into his neighborhood.

Like the rage that engulfed me whenever our black-and-white television set succumbed to age and a fat, moving black line fixed itself on the screen.

Like the explosion of possibilities that accompanied those quiet moments when my mother asked me to recite the alphabet, to say a new word, to repeat my full name and street address, or to count higher than I had previously.

Like the private satisfaction generated by an imagination that saw faces and bodies in the patterns of the cheap, brown-and-beige kitchen chairs.

And like the sheer delight and obscure passing of tradition when my mother taught me to do "the jerk," "the mashed potato," or "the twist," or when she belted the lyrics to a Smokey Robinson or Marvin Gaye song....

1995

KEVIN POWELL

Jersey City |

73

Son2Mother

Mother, have I told you
That you are the first woman
I ever fell in love with, that what
I've always wanted in life is to hear
You say you love me, too?

That is why, ma, it has taken
Me so long to write this poem.
For how could I, a
Grown man, put words to paper
If I am that little boy
Cowering beneath the power of
That slap, the swing of that belt,
Or the slash and burn of that switch
You used to beat me into fear and submission?

I constantly cringe, ma,
When I think of that oft-repeated chorus you sung
As a fusillade of blows walloped my skeleton body:
Are you gonna be good? Are you gonna be good?
Sometimes when I call you these days, mother,
I just don't know what to say, thus I fall silent,
Even when you ask "How are you doing?"
I want to give you real talk,
Tell you that I am still that stunted only child
Traumatized by the violence of your voice;
That I am still that shorty too terrified to fall
Asleep for fear of your pouncing on me
The moment I shut my eyes—
And you did, mother, again and again,
Until I could no longer sleep peacefully
As a child, and I have never actually had
Many tranquil nights of sleep since.
I lay awake sometimes, as an adult,
Thinking someone is going to get me,
Going to strike me, going to kill me
Because of those heart-racing hours
Of darkness far far ago.

And I remember that time I ran under
Our bed, and in your titanic rage
You tore the entire bed apart,
The frame falling on one of my legs,
And there I was, stuck, mother,
And you ripped into me anyhow.
And oh how I howled for mercy.
But there was none, mother.
Yet there was that chorus:
Are you gonna be good? Are you gonna be good?
And I really did not know, mother, what being good meant.
Nor what you wanted me to be.
Because one day I thought you loved me
And the next day I thought you hated me.

And I did not know back in the day, ma,
That you had been assaulted and abused
The same way, by my granddaddy,
Your father, a 19th century son of ex-slaves
who would break you and your
Three sisters and brother down with mule whips,
With soda bottles, with his gnarled hands—
That he was an embittered mister,
That you were the child who became
Most like your father. Do you not
Recall that past, mother?
I am saying you once chided me,
After you learned I had struck someone as an adult,
To keep my hands to myself, and I wanted to say
But, ma, why didn't you keep your hands to yourself?
Why didn't you command your hands, your arms,
To hug me, instead of urging them to damage me?

And that is what I previously was, ma: damaged
Goods that liked living on the other side of midnight.
That is why, mother, there was no sleep for me till Brooklyn,
Because I needed to escape the concrete box
Needed to escape the mental terrorism
Needed to escape you and that
Paranoid schizophrenic existence.

KEVIN POWELL

Son2Mother |

75

I am not crazy, ma. I know
Our destinies were frozen in those days
When we shared
That bed and room together,
Because we were too poor
To afford a full apartment.
To those days, mother, when I
Thought you were the bravest
Human being on earth as you
Fought super-sized black rats with
Your broomstick, or effortlessly
Shooed the army of roaches away
From our dinner table—

Maybe, ma, I have not been
Able to write this poem
Because I can envision you as a
Young mother, the one who suitcased
Her dreams when you left South
Carolina, when you moved, first, to Miami
To create a new life for yourself, to flee
The world that murdered your
Grandfather, a local cook, by stuffing food in his mouth,
Then baptizing him in cracker water and proclaiming
It was an accident. It was the world that knocked
On your grandmother's door and told
Her she had to give up 397 of those 400 acres
Of land called the Powell Property—
One penny for each acre of land—
And what your grandmother was left with
Was a jar of soil called Shoe Hill,
The contaminated hill where you were born, ma:
That world never bothered to change the
Name from the Powell Property. And there you
Were, at age eight, sunrising with the moldy men
And the wash-and-wear women
As God's yawn and morning stretch

Tickled the rooster's neck,
Waking you good colored folks to toil on that Powell Property—
To pick cotton for White folks as if being
Cheap and exploited labor was your American birthright.

And you were angry bye and bye, mother.
You would get so angry, Aunt Birdie told me
One time, that sweat droplets would form on your nose,
Your brow would curl up, and the world and
Anyone in it would become your
Empty lard can to kick back and forth up the road a piece.
Ah, ma, but you were such a pretty little Black
Girl—I have the picture right here this minute,
Of you at 12 or 13, tender and dark ebony skin
A beautiful yet temperamental and unloved Black girl
Told that you were ugly, that you had ugly hair,
That you would never be anything other than
The help and wooden steps for someone else's climb—

But you were persistent, ma, and mad determined
To make something of yourself.
And Jersey City
Welcomed you as it welcomed each of
The lost-found children of the Old South
Welcomed y'all country cousins to
Number runners slumlords
Pimps drug dealers bad credit
Huge debts and would-be
Prophets who called themselves storefront preachers
And there you were, mother, within a year,
With my father—

Was he your first love, ma, did he mop
The Carolina clay from your feet?
Did he sprinkle sweet tea and lemon on your belly?
Did he ever really make love to you, mother?
Or was he more like that plantation robot
Who was built to mate then make a quick
Dash to the next slave quarters?

KEVIN POWELL

Son2Mother

What I do know, mother, is that you went to the hospital
Alone, to spread your legs for
A doctor whose plasma face you do not remember
To push forth a seed you had attempted
To destroy twice because you feared his
Birth would mean the death of you.
But there I was, ma, in your arms
Screaming lunging fleeing
And you were so tremendously ashamed
To be an unwed mother that you did
Not tell Grandma Lottie for five years,
Until that day we showed up
In your hometown of Ridgeland, South Carolina.

But what a mother you were:
You taught me to talk
Taught me to know my name
Taught me to count to read to think
To aspire to be something.
You, my grade-school educated mother,
Gave me my swagger—
Told me I was going to be a lawyer or a doctor,
Told me I was going to do big things,
That I was going to have a better life
Than this welfare this food stamp this government cheese
Had pre-ordained for us.
And we prayed, mother, yes lawd we prayed—
To that God in the sky, to the White Jesus on our wall,
To the minister with the good hair and the tailored suits,
To the minister with the gift
To chalk on busted souls and spit game in foreign tongues—
And back then, ma, I did not understand the talking in tongues
The need to pin pieces of prayer cloth on our attire
The going to church twice a week
The desperation to phone prayer hotlines when there was trouble.
But what you were doing, ma,
Was stapling our paper lives together as best you could
Making a way out of no way

Especially after my father announced,
When I was eight,
That he would not give "a near nickel" to us again.
And he never did, mother, never—

And I sometimes wonder if that is when
The attacks got worse because you were
So viciously wounded
By my father's ignorance and brutality
That that ignorance and brutality
Was transferred to me
As you would say, in one breath,
Don't be like your father
And in another
You just like your no-good daddy

And, yes, I am crying this second, mother,
As I write this poem
Because I see you today:
A retired Black woman with a limp, a bad leg,
Shuffling up and down three flights of stairs.
Too headstrong to allow me to move
You from that heat-less apartment,
Life reduced to trips to the grocery store
A bus ride to the mall
A sacred pilgrimage to the laundry room
And the daily ritual of judge shows, Oprah, and the local news.

And, mother, you remain without the love you forever
Crave, and you forever speak of getting married one day.
And you are so very worn out from
Fifty-four years of back breaking work—
But this I know now:
Your life was sacrificed so that I could have one, ma.

So I write this poem, son to mother, to say I love you
Even if you refuse to accept my words
Because you are too afraid to defeat the devil
And bury the past with our ancestors once and for all.

I write this poem
To say I forgive you for everything, mother—
For the poverty for the violence for the hunger
For the loneliness for the fear
For the days when I blamed you for my absent father
For the days when I wanted to run away
For those days when I really did run away—
I forgive you, ma, for those days you cursed
And belittled me, for those days when you said
I was never gonna make it.
Oh, yes, ma, I do forgive, I forgive you for
The beatings, I do, dear mother, I do—
Because if it were not for all of who you are
All of where you come from
All of what you created for me
I would not be alive today.

For below the bloody scar tissues of your fire and fury
And aggravations and self-imposed house arrest
Is a woman who defied the mythmakers
Turned her nose up at the doomsayers—
Is someone who fought landlords
And crooked police officers and
Social workers and school systems and
Deadbeat men who wanted to live off of
Her; and from the tar and feathered remains
Of lives noosed from the very beginning,
We have survived, and here we are, mother:
You have never said you love me
But I know every time I come home
And you've made potato salad and stringbeans,
Every year you've mailed me a birthday card
Or asked if you should buy me pajamas for Christmas,
I know that you are,
In your own wildly unpredictable way,
The greatest love I've ever had in my life—

Tuesday, January 1, 2008
8:28AM

 | Son2Mother

Publication Credits

Some of these poems/pieces have previously appeared in *Konch, Long Shot, Aloud: Voices from the Nuyorican Poets Café, Essence, African Voices, Drumvoices Revue, Bum Rush The Page: A Def Poetry Jam,* www.defpoetryjam.com, *Eyeball, Vibe,* Drylongso.com, *In The Tradition: An Anthology of Young Black Writers, recognize, Sable, Step Into A World: A Global Anthology of The New Black Literature, Rolling Out,* SeeingBlack.com, *Role Call: A Generational Anthology of Social and Political Black Literature & Art,* www.MTV.com, www.tbwt.org, *Someday We'll All Be Free,* www.iveknownrivers.org (The Museum of the African Diaspora's website), www.literafeelyamagazine.net, www.daveyd.com, *From Totems To Hip Hop,* and the Scottsdale Museum of Contemporary Art ("HairStories" exhibit, in collaboration with painter Radcliffe Bailey).

About the poet

Kevin Powell, poet, essayist, public speaker, college lecturer, political activist, hiphop historian, and businessman, was born and raised in Jersey City, New Jersey. He has resided in Brooklyn, New York, for nearly two decades, where he has written or edited all eight of his books, including *No Sleep Till Brooklyn.* He can be contacted at kevin@kevinpowell.net.